MW01673501

THE FAITHFUL SERVANT

A TRUE STORY OF MY JOURNEY WITH GOD

NATHAN DYER

Unless otherwise noted, all Bible verses have been taken from the New Living Translation of the Holy Bible

Printed in the United States of America

ISBN: 978-0-578-90842-7 (paperback)

ISBN: 978-0-578-90843-4 (ebook)

TABLE OF CONTENTS

SPECIAL THANKS

I would like to give a special thanks first to God, Pastor Steven Furtick and family, Elevation Church, T.D. Jakes and family and every church all over the world. I love you all.

To all the brothers and sisters Richard Washington from Columbia, SC, Sarah Hall from Jamaica, Jaleel Tucker from Guys Hill St. Catherine, Jamaica, Sergio Sanchez from Barstow, California, Luke Parker from PA.

To all the wonderful people over there just making wonderful movies, you know who you are. Hugs and music!

I'd like to thank my fantastic Elevation e-group members in Freedom Fighters, Victory & Recovery in Jesus, and Chain breakers.

An incredibly special thanks to the greatest author coach ever to live, Jacinda Estelle, in Waco, Texas, and the owner of Value in Care Specialties, LLC.

To every single person alive, I love you all!

INTRODUCTION

I give my savior Jesus Christ all the credit for putting the right people in my life for this book to come to pass.

I want to clarify that I would not have made it through my trials and tribulations without God in my life.

I definitely would not have had the courage to publish this true story. So many people go through life lost and stay lost, not realizing that the answer to mental health is right in front of them. The answer is God's Word.

A joyful, wonderful, and peaceful life awaits you. I pray this book encourages people to connect with God, the only one who truly can help. Salvation is free.

Luke 10:19 says, "Look, I have given you authority over all the power of the enemy, and you can walk among snakes and scorpions and crush them. Nothing will injure you."

Luke 10:20 says, "But don't rejoice because evil spirits obey you; rejoice because your names are registered in heaven."

Colossians 3:15 says, “And let the peace that comes from Christ rule in your hearts. For as members of one body, you are called to live in peace. And always be thankful.”

John 14:27 says, “I am leaving you with a gift - peace of mind and heart. And the peace I give is a gift the world cannot give. So don’t be troubled or afraid.”

CHAPTER 1

FAMILY LIFE

Hello, I am Nathan Dyer. I was born in the small town of Moline, Illinois, on June 30, 1982.

This is my life, a true story. I hope God blesses you like He did me in June 2020. I am thirty-eight years old, five foot eleven. I am half Caucasian and half Mexican because my mom is Caucasian, which leaves my father, who is Mexican.

Before I tell this story, I would like to start by saying that my mother is twenty-three years sober, and my older sister is the best mom you could ever ask for. You will understand why I say that later on in my story. I love all my family so much. Though my dad is an alcoholic, he saved my life. I know God will help him because I will never stop praying for him. My brother deals with his addiction to drugs. My dad and my brothers are natural-born fighters, and I love them both very much!

Okay, so here we go! I want you to know drudging up one's past is difficult, and it is difficult for anyone to write about their story. I wrote this to heal and provide hope to people that have been through much trauma in life and feel hopeless. After you read my story, you may even feel motivated to go to church! If so, praise

God! Jesus is ready to help you. He is just waiting on you to say yes.

My earliest memory is around two years old (funny how I can remember that far back), still in diapers. I sat by a deep body of water that was eight feet deep. The next thing I know, I was drowning. An African American boy swooped in and saved my life. Right then, I was sure he was an angel sent from heaven. Matthew 4:6 says, and said, "If you are the Son of God, jump off! For the Scriptures say, 'He will order his angels to protect you. And they will hold you up with their hands so you won't even hurt your foot on a stone.

Then, at three years old, I was outside on one of those plastic three-wheelers for kids. I do not remember if I was unsupervised, but I tried to cross the street and got hit and run over by a car my neighbor was driving. I remember my mother sneaking me chocolate when the doctor said I should not eat. Thanks, mom!

These are the only memories I have before we moved to Georgia. We moved when I was five years old, and I only saw my dad a few times until the age of ten. My mom was not around very much, but they did the best they knew how. It is not like raising kids comes with a manual.

Well, as a kid, my first thought or lie from the devil was that no one would ever love me, especially if my own parents did not. John 8:44 says, "For you are the children of your father the devil, and you love to do the evil things he does. He was a murderer from the beginning. He has always hated the truth because there is no truth in him. When he lies, it is consistent with his character; for he is a liar and the father of lies." This was a devastating thought for a child to have! The devil will lie to you and have you working for him as early as he can!

My twelve-year-old sister had to watch over us many times because my parents stayed gone. I remember not washing dishes for my sister, and she chased me into the woods, and I ended up staying there for the rest of the day. She does not remember doing that to this day. I would have to go in the house at night-time because I was not that brave to spend the entire night outside by myself. My mom did not come home, and I still had to deal with my sister. Similar to an elephant back then, she forgot nothing. She would still beat me up for not washing the dishes. Luke 12:52 says, "From now on families will be split apart, three in favor of me, and two against—or two in favor and three against."

At this point, I thought family should love you, but again the devil told me they did not. Such a crushing blow to the mind! Now, there were those rare occasions when my parents were finally home at the same time. They would fight, yell, and throw each other's belongings. What really hurt was when mom grabbed something out of my hand. It was a gift I had gotten her, and she flung it at my dad's head. Watch out, dad! The gift shattered, and tears rolled down my face like the mighty Mississippi River.

One day my mother came home with a black eye, and she could hardly move. The incident occurred with her best friend, alcohol, a tree, and a day spent in jail, nothing like tearing families apart. During this time, a lady named Sandra came to watch us. She was not a pleasant person and would hit us for not eating all our food. I remember my younger brother getting hit most of the time. If we talked while she was watching television, she would yell and then punish us by locking us in our rooms. No child should go through such trauma!

Devastating memories continued for me at eight when my fourteen-year-old cousin, Jess, was watching us. Unfortunately, Jess's mother liked alcohol too much, and Jess was just a child herself and did not know how to take care of kids.

One day my cousin and I experimented with kicking out the under bracing of a California king waterbed. Having no parents around, can you guess what happened next? The bed fell on my left leg. My sister ran to the neighbors to call 911. I do not remember who gave me a butter knife, but I started stabbing it, and out came the water. My cousin and I lifted it off my leg as the fire department showed up.

Family time spent together at Christmas was not all bad. My favorite gifts were the Nintendo basketball, including a 55-gallon trash container I used as my hoop, then we upgraded to a milk crate and my four-foot teddy bear. When I was eight and needed a baseball glove, I begged my mom to get one for me, but she forgot. Just recently, I finally got over it; like really, what was wrong with me?

I considered myself a messed-up kid. There was a time I watched my brother get whipped for sniffing the gas in my father's prized silver Mustang that was not in the best shape. I watched my younger brother get beat, and it was difficult to watch because it was mentally challenging. Around nine years of age, my mother got a new boyfriend, and the boys could not stay, so they shipped us off with my dad, who we had only been around a few times in our entire lives. I fell into believing the lie my mind told me that my mom did not want us.

CHAPTER 2

THE PLANTED SEED

When we first moved to Illinois, we stayed at my dad's mom's house, which would make her my grandma, but now she is one of my angels. She planted the first seed when she introduced me to Jesus. We had to go to church, and let us be honest, at nine, I did not want to be there, but I thank God now she instilled that in me.

Despite of that seed planted, I felt like a destroyed little individual. I had seven Latina aunts and a grandma. If I dared to talk back, I would get beat up by one of my two professional boxing uncles. I learned quickly to respect ladies, and I thank my uncles for that. They were well known around the Quad Cities, Jesus El Toro Correa and Ferocious Feliciano Correa. My boxing skills came from watching my uncles, so I joined a boxing club. I think it is good for a person to learn to defend themselves if it teaches them responsibility and only use it when they need it.

I met some boxers like Lonnie Horn, who is not as famous. Roy Jones Jr. is another boxer I met before he became famous. When my uncles had to fight at boxing events, I remember seeing Butter-bean fight, and I cherished those memories. People would rather watch two people knock their heads off instead of reading a book and getting knowledge. Hosea 4:6 says, “My people are being destroyed because they don’t know me. Since you priests refuse to know me, I refuse to recognize you as my priests. Since you have forgotten the laws of your God, I will forget to bless your children.” If you notice, a lot of our young kids are going to jail now!

My dad met some lady we ended up moving in with, and our church routine stopped. However, I already learned to pray, so I prayed for my family, myself, and the entire world every night. I could not go to bed unless I did. That lady and my dad grew close, and she became my stepmother, but unfortunately, my dad liked the booze too much, and yet again, we were yelled at and had items thrown at us. I was becoming used to pain and fear. Leviticus 10:9 says, “You and your descendants must never drink wine or any other alcoholic drink before going into the Tabernacle. If you do, you will die. This is a permanent law for you, and it must be observed from generation to generation.

My stepmother changed her attitude toward us and began mistreating us with frequent whippings, and she was not like that when we first met her. She would make us pick our own hickory switch, also known as a little thin branch, that went right through our jeans. I am sure some of you all know what that feels like.

Lots of fun, right? Just kidding, these were obviously not fun times, but that was our life. We got punished for simple things like being five minutes late from the baseball diamonds, and they left nice red marks on your legs. My brother and I were walking to school one morning, and there was a truck pulling a smaller boat that we did not see at first. I was on my bike, and my brother walked right past the truck, and the front of the boat hit him on the head.

My mind went into a frazzled state, and I rode home as fast as I could to tell our dad. No one should ever experience what I saw with my brother getting flown to Iowa City hospital. Again, I say no kid should go through such trauma. I know so many have seen worse, but I was a kid. He immediately had to get surgery to have his two lower ribs removed, they fused his neck, and he stayed in the hospital for eight months. During this time, he became pleasantly plump, had a halo drilled into his head, and the doctor prescribed pain medication which paved the way to his drug addiction. Thank God for the good old Ronald McDonald house because we lived a long way away and could stay at the hospital while he went through this traumatic event.

The real reason he needed to have this surgery is because when he was two years old, our home caught on fire, and my dad was around (Thank God!). He had to lower us out the window, but unfortunately, he dropped my brother on his head, so his neck muscles deteriorated. God knew my brother needed this surgery. Six years later, he was in boxing when the boat hit him, and his doctor said that if it had hit him any worse, it could have paralyzed him.

Though my dad had a drinking problem, these were the best four years of my childhood because of how active I was. I learned to play baseball, basketball, and football for a short time. I was a small kid, so football was not for me, and I knew that immediately. It only took one concussion for me to realize that. My dad even taught us how to fish, and I still love fishing to this day.

My favorite part of these years was when I got to spend time at my cousin's house playing video games, computer games, and eating free Frank's Pizza in Silvis, Illinois, which my uncle owned. Before my grandma became one of my angels, we had family get-togethers all the time. This is a significant part of Mexican culture. I just want to say thanks again, Grandma, for introducing me to my Savior, Jesus Christ, I love you so very much, and I know you are reading this from heaven.

The family get-togethers always involved my dad getting into a fight with my Aunt Lupe or anyone else, resulting in us leaving early and cutting our fun short as if they did not damage us enough. Around this time, I was thirteen, getting whipped for several things by my stepmother, but at least she taught me to fold my clothes after washing them, and I am grateful for that, just not all the red marks on my legs.

Because of the red marks, I was the only guy wearing jeans in gym class, and I felt weird and out of place, but I made it through with points off my grade. I didn't want the other kids to see the marks on my legs. My teacher did not appreciate how I refused to dress out, but I learned to play basketball very well.

That year my uncle drove up from Georgia to pick up one of my cousins. My mom was dating someone new, and the opportunity was available where I could move back to Georgia with my mom. So, in the middle of the night, not thinking at all what it would do to my eight-year-old brother, who always had his big brother with him, I left with my uncle. I did not find out what this had done to him emotionally and mentally until I was thirty-six years old. This was devastating for me. It triggered an overwhelming sense of responsibility for the destruction of his life and the things he still struggles with to this day. I cried and cried because it hurts me so badly when I think about it.

I had to leave a few of my friends back in Illinois, where I encountered my bully. His name was Todd, granted he was much bigger than I, and I believe he repeated a few grades. I stood up to him one day when I kicked him in his legs, and of course, I took off running because courage and lack of intelligence are two entirely different things. We became friends after that incident and started playing basketball during every recess.

I also left my best friend behind. We did everything together, like shooting hoops. This was when I fell in love with Michael Jordan as so many did. I would spend hours outside practicing Jordan's patient, fade away in all four of the defenders' faces and make the shoot. It was a sweet play! Now, I was back in Georgia with my mother, and I knew I should have been happy, but I was not. I still considered myself to be a dysfunctional child.

CHAPTER 3

STRONG INSECURITIES

My mom was dating an African American man named Mike. He was a big Christian and an exceptional guy. This was my second introduction to Jesus, but I was still a child and understood little about God; I just knew I prayed to him. Well, my mom was also battling with alcohol, and she probably regretted some mistakes from the past, so she allowed me to do as I pleased. As long as I called to let her know where I was, then it was okay. Eventually, I stopped doing it because I lied to her twice, and I felt too horrible. I did not realize the pain I was inflicting on her. And I ask God to forgive me all the time for my egregious actions. What that must have done to her, having to stay up all night wondering if her kids were still alive. Exodus 20:5 says, "You must not bow down to them or worship them, for I, the LORD your God, am a jealous God who will not tolerate your affection for any other gods. I lay the sins of the parents upon their children; the entire family is affected - even children in the third and fourth generations of those who reject me." We bring destruction upon ourselves and future generations by not following God's Word.

Right before I turned fourteen, I got my first job busting tables at a restaurant, and my mom knew the bartender she could get me a job. This girl asked me out to the movies, and of course, I said yes. By this point, I was so messed up, people-pleasing was normal for me to feel accepted because of the abandonment issues I was dealing with.

My mom was the assistant manager; her boyfriend was the manager at the theater in the mall. I was excited because at thirteen years old, I had my money, and that was cool. I do not remember the name of the girl who asked me out, just that she was from Boston. She had a sexy accent. She would pick me up and take me to the movies. We ended up at Lake Lanier when it was dark. The girl was around twenty, and I was almost fourteen. She grabbed my private area, and I cannot say that I had any complaints, so you can imagine what happened next. Yep, we had sex, but I did not know at the time they called this statutory rape. Back then, there was a stigma that boys did not get raped, and people would ridicule male victims for saying they did. I did not have a great relationship with my mother or father, so I internalized my hurt and blamed myself.

When puberty hit, I had a happy little trail down yonder, and shaving became part of my routine. With no one to teach me about shaving or going against the grain to prevent razor bumps, I did not have the best personal hygiene ritual. Besides, my body changes, the sweating causing an unpleasant smell, then came the itching from cheap detergent; the term I learned is hypoallergenic, but we bought whatever detergent we could afford, I guess.

With hormones raging and hygiene issues combined with sexual assault resulted in once again the devil lying to me. My brain automatically told me I had an S.T.D. and that I was ugly, nasty, and disgusting. The things our brains tell us can make or break us. The devil had his paws tightly secure around me because I already thought that no one could ever love me. I thought this because the devil told me my own parents did not love me. Talk about being chained up in the mind! It would ultimately take God to remove those chains. I was so ashamed, and I did not have a good relationship with my parents, so my life seemed pretty much over at thirteen.

I had smoked marijuana a couple of times, but this is when the drug use became heavy. I was smoking over fourteen grams a day just to be okay with myself. This event in my life started a twenty-two-year battle with addiction for me that eventually progressed into other, harder drugs. The event destroyed my life, and up to this point, I was so very lost. My advice to those struggling with drug addiction is: Please avoid this at all costs. Do not let the devil lie to you. Our focus cannot be on the lie that we need drugs to cope.

Then came the confidence issue of talking to or being around women. Of course, as a young boy at thirteen, you have these raging hormones, and I discovered porn, and sadly, a new addiction was born. The shame and guilt of being a drug addict prevented me from visiting a family much. I lived in Georgia for about a year and a half and only visited my grandma, Pearlene, one time for about ten minutes. Then God took her home. Knowing I had so many opportunities to see her devastated and utterly haunted me for a couple of decades. However, the shame was too great because of the drug usage. This is where my life kind of went in two different directions simultaneously. I gained many of the wrong friends in school and could get marijuana cheap, so I sold drugs too. God, please forgive me for such foolish acts. Acts 16:30-31 says, "Then he brought them out and asked, "Sirs, what must I do to be saved?" They replied, "Believe in the Lord Jesus and you will be saved, along with everyone in your household."

After six months of bussing tables, I moved on and worked at the movie theatre where my mom and Mike worked putting movies together. I worked there for about two years and learned all the job positions. Somehow, I graduated high school, so God, I give you all the glory for that miracle. After that, I started working at Domino's Pizza, where I became a manager-in-training for two more years.

My mind was not on being with a woman because of my past, so I focused on making money while my friends focused on girls. The money came so fast that the marijuana usage became all day, every day. Partying was a fixture in my daily routine with my so-called group of around thirty friends, but I would part ways when the girls come around, I guess because my experience with women was just hurt.

Though I was antisocial with women, I ended up having my first girlfriend named Erica. She was the most beautiful blonde-haired girl I had ever met, so what she saw in me was beyond my comprehension. I was so messed up already that I could not even connect dots to think she liked me. Drugs will do that to a person.

I struggled to think I was handsome because the devil already had his hold on me. We dated for a year and a half. Her mom loved me, to my surprise. Who likes their daughter dating anyone? But she eventually cheated on me. I guess because she wanted what my brain would not allow me to engage in -- sex. Remember my brain told me I was ugly, no one would ever love me, and I had an S.T.D. But I could tell no one or deal with the problem. I was too ashamed.

You can imagine the negative headspace I was in by now. There was a two-week span where I could not find marijuana. Two weeks without marijuana! That was the end of the world for me. When that door closed, here came Xanax knocking, and I allowed this drug right into my life. Forgetting life became simpler now, and I had plenty of money. Drugs and money did not seem to stop coming.

Since my only goal in life was to forget about everything, the drugs made that happen by altering my brain, and I lost four days by not remembering anything. Here is the kicker, though, being twenty-five to thirty-five minutes from Atlanta, drugs were cheap and accessible. Probably a third of my life I do not even remember, and only God knows the things I may have done, so please forgive me, Jesus.

My problem was that I would start off buying a few, and before I knew it, I was eating sixteen milligrams a night. This is a progressive disease, and I quickly found that out, but it allowed me to forget my truth, which was a lie. Besides losing days, losing things became common. The worst thing is the unhappiness that overwhelmed me for so many reasons, but most of all, loneliness.

CHAPTER 4
FAITH EMERGED

God made His first major appearance in my life at eighteen. I had plenty of money but lost my job, so one day, I headed to the tire shop to get two new tires. On my way to get tires, I prayed, thanking God for everything in my life. I asked God if He could find me a job, and before I could even say in, "Jesus' name, Amen," my phone started ringing. I answered my phone, and it was my buddy, Nick:

> "What's up?" I asked.
> "Nothing," he said. "What are you doing tomorrow?"
> I told him, "I am not doing anything."
> He said, "Do you want to come work in the morning?"
> "Of course!" I said yes and hung up the phone.

Mark 11:24 says, "I tell you, you can pray for anything, and if you believe that you've received it, it will be yours."

I could not believe what just happened, but I thanked God! From that moment, my faith was born. I knew I could talk to Him like I talk to anyone else. Gratefulness covered my heart because I was alone most of the time and was unhappy. No one ever knew about this because I thought it was just for me to understand. I had not even read the Bible because I figured why read it if God just answers my prayers? Who knew I would share my blessing with the entire world through this book!

I began talking to the Lord more often, but I was so messed up it became only when I needed Him like most of us do. I would just talk to God like I am to you. Thank you, God, for that blessing of knowing that I could talk to you because I needed it.

Trouble with the law became my next challenge. There I was, driving drunk. Then, *boom.* D.U.I! After twenty-five hundred dollars later, I did not even have to go into the courtroom. Five years later, I got another D.U.I., and this time issues began flooding in. Before I knew it, I was on four different probations. Here comes drug certificate, after drug certificate, then sobriety. It was the first time I got sober. Believe it or not, I got through all four probations. That was an incredibly stressful time in my life, but I believe everything happens for a reason, so I thank God for the trials.

You would think I had learned my lesson by now, but oh no! As the saying goes, things were just getting ready to hit the fan! I felt so bad about myself that I was consuming any drug you could think of, and because the money kept coming in, I had no shortage of supply. Throughout this period of my life, I was so dead inside that there were several occasions my youngest sister and I would just get into arguments. I think I was just being hardheaded. There were three or four times I survived being stabbed by a steak knife. Dodging death became a daily activity, and I was pretty good at it.

I started in the construction industry for work, starting off with vinyl siding, gutters, painting, and framing. After having so many years in the industry, I had helped in every stage of building a house by the time I quit construction. My uncle was the mastermind for building homes, and I just learned as much as I could with him.

Now, here comes a little action-adventure for you. Some friends and I went out, and it was thirteen of us in a small S-10 truck going down East Hall Road where I grew up. The truck tires touched a piece of grass and slid sideways, going off the road. The truck went flipping six times down a twenty-foot cliff. Thank God it was cold.

I fell out on the very first flip because I had my arms and hands inside of my shirt to stay warm. I more than likely would have grabbed the side of the truck had it been warm, and it would have been a different story. God saved me, plus because of the cold weather, I did not feel any pain. I ended up with a few scratches, and I got up and ran to my aunt's house, which was about a mile away, and called 911. A friend of mine went to jail because they found a gun. Yes, these were the type of people I was hanging out with and the world I lived in.

Around the age of twenty-one, I had a couple of ladies who apparently did not like that I was not hitting on them or trying to have sex with them. They knew I liked Xanax and gave me a bunch of them, and I accepted them. I cannot really blame them for what happened next. When I could no longer move, they took what I would not consent to giving them. I take the blame for putting myself in that position. This happened several more times, and it is sad the acts some people do when they take advantage of someone in an unhealthy mental state.

I went back to Domino's for about six months. This is when I meant Leah, the first woman that did not just want to sleep with me. She was a breath of fresh air, beautiful, soft, and radiant, and I really like her a lot. Here was the problem: To this point, I did not have the excellent communication skills to be in a relationship with women.

There were very few women I would talk to outside of the family. The only conversations I had were seemingly with women who wanted sex, and by God, they would take it. This would be the second time God shows up in my life. I turned to God for my lack of so-called swag. I just did not have the "pop my collar skills," so I prayed, thanking Him again for everything He had given me. Then I continued in prayer, "God, if Leah likes me, please give me a sign," and it was not fifteen seconds after I prayed my phone pinged a text message, and it was Leah asking me to come pick her up.

I seriously could not believe what just happened. I looked up, saying, "Thank you, God!" I remember feeling the first bit of genuine joy in my heart. She also was the first person to buy me a birthday gift (I had not received a gift since I was twelve years old). She was an outstanding person to me.

One day, I was on my way to pick her up from her job, and she wanted to drive, so I agreed because it was only five minutes away. She was getting her license the next day, and I thought it would help her. I thought wrong, and she ended up wrecking the car. Thankfully, God had a tree stop us from going into a little river.

After the wreck, she told me she had a few drinks. Lord Jesus! When the cop showed up, I told him I was driving. They searched me, found a pack of tobacco-rolling papers you can buy at any gas station, and charged me with my third D.U.I. Thank God there were five years between the first two of my past charges. Fortunately, they charged me like it was my second.

None of that mattered to me. The only thing I cared about was that Leah was okay and not in any trouble. She showed me love when I did not even know how to love myself. Her mom came to get me out of jail and made Leah give me her car, which I was grateful for because she was not letting her get her license the next day. Definitely a smart move! Her car was not as nice as mine, but that was okay because at least I still had a car.

CHAPTER 5

YOUNG AND LOST

That morning they activated this new stoplight on this sharp curve in the road. I was going too fast and hit a Cadillac Escalade. They asked if I was okay, and I knew they were, so I took off. They chased us, but I turned on a gravel road, and it became too dusty for them to continue. These are the critically dumb decisions you make when the devil has a total grip on your life. You could bet your bottom dollar I had drugs on me, and I was not proud of myself at all.

I got back to my mother's house feeling relieved. A few hours later, I took off. Yes, you guessed it, to go sell drugs. The police caught up to me, pulled me over, and I had about twenty guns pointed at me. You want to talk about intense. You could not have fit a needle up there! So, it was off to jail for the second time in one day. I am so blessed because it could have been much worse. The cops never found the drugs. One cop said, "We let you go this morning, and you are back already!" I got out of jail and did not sell hard drugs anymore as if any drug is okay to sell.

I was young and lost, so here come more certificates and more probation, but little did I know some even tougher obstacles were soon to come up. It was not long after this heartache that another devastating event occurred. We had seen my Aunt Joan, who we hardly ever got to see. She was smiling in her new Mustang; it was nice. The following weekend, they found her hung and called it a suicide.

This is another one of those events that could just destroy anyone, and it did for me. I attended her funeral the following week; I had to turn myself into jail for eight months, and it was tough for me. Get this. We are so poor that her ashes went into plastic bags, and these were times when I wished God would just take me out. I was twenty-four years old, and I needed God again. I wanted my life back; I wanted to be okay. The only way I knew to be okay was to always say yes to people that asked me for money. The problem was it was a temporary joy, but I needed that joy to live. I prayed, "God, please help me get my life back on track!"

Now God does not always give you what you ask for in the way you might think. He gives you what you need. God knew what I needed after ten years. They caught me with drugs and were looking at giving me a fifteen-year prison sentence. It was my first major drug offense, and it was not a matter of IF I am going, but WHEN I would be going. I had to clean up my act at this moment of my life.

Since it was my first major offense, they offered me drug court, and I got out on a signature bond and had to report right away. This was the beginning of a hard-fought twenty-five months, but well worth it. It taught me tools on how to get sober but staying sober takes help from God. I would have to attend classes, AA, NA meetings, and court. At one point, I had to take sixteen drug tests in fourteen days: it was teaching me to be accountable for sure.

For the first time, I could smile without drugs. It did not last because of my mental scarring from the sexual abuse. My brain still believed that I was filthy and ugly, so I went back to drug usage. I was so blessed financially; I had gained a lot of pleasant things. Two D.U.I.'s the following year after drug court had me on another spiral downhill. I had to take eighteen more months of classes by this time; I had so many certificates it was just sad.

At this point, I had lost almost everything: my cars, three-bedroom lake view apartment, clothes, shoes, and cash. It boiled down to around ninety-thousand dollars (sigh, just money, right?). I was required to take drug treatment classes that lasted three and a half more years. If I added up all the classes that I took in the past, including now, that is a total of five years. The ultimate consequence is landing in jail more times than I can count. I am not proud of this, which is why I am writing. Even if I only help one person, then writing this book is worth it. Some of my experiences were overdosing maybe four times and even waking up in jail in a hospital gown. It is not a good life when you live being controlled by the devil. God, I pray you help one person to avoid this lifestyle with this book.

I also want to let you know God loves you and will save you if you have faith and allow him to. This is when I finally quit selling drugs. I am so thankful for God because now I would not have to always be looking over my shoulder for cops. I know some of you know exactly what I am talking about. During my ten-year construction adventure, I had fallen twenty-three feet, and another time, I fell sixteen feet, so thank God I had started another job in the printing industry. I printed on poly and cryovac film but then lost that job because of a D.U.I and jail time. To my surprise, I got a job printing the Gainesville Times newspaper. Boy, that was a messy job!

One day I went on vacation and ended up at the wrong house. Just my luck, it was a meth house! There it was: meth, one of the purest forms of the devil you can find. After ten years of not seeing this drug, there it was. I went straight downhill. I lost my job and met an abusive woman, and I had so-called friends stealing from me whenever they found the opportunity.

One friend I knew for seven years took four thousand dollars from me. The other friend I knew for twelve years took two thousand dollars. These were friends I used to trust, but after I got away from them, I quit helping people or trusting people. The guy I knew for twelve years had his girlfriend drug me, and when I came to, I was being thrown down a flight of sixty steps in Atlanta left for dead. I had to run around for an hour with my elbow facing up, trying to convince someone to take me to the hospital.

A week later, I encountered a nineteen-year-old associate (because I did not consider anyone a friend). Two days after I saw him, I called him and found out that he had taken his own life with a gun. I liked the kid. That is a tough feeling.

God was about to fix all my addictions after the reintroducing of the devil into my life because, in my mind, that is what meth was. The egregious acts that many years of porn and drug addiction caused keeps me from going back to that life.

CHAPTER 6

GOING BACK WITH A CHANGED MIND

One day, I was on my way home, and I bumped into a boat propeller and wrecked my car. The cop was nice until he saw my past, and then I was tried, convicted, and guilty in his mind. I told him about my empty marijuana pipe, just to be honest. Well, he asked me twenty questions in ten minutes. I had only been up five minutes. He did not find any drugs or alcohol, but because I answered the same question a little differently, he arrested me and charged me with another D.U.I.

I ended up waiting to hear from the court. By the time I was summoned, I was almost homeless and broke, but I went. They told me I did not have any court dates and to go home to call the clerk of courts. So, I did, and they told me the same thing: no court dates. I asked them what I should do, and they said to live my life.

My dad offered me a bus ticket back to Moline, Illinois. I had not seen this place in sixteen years. It was a chance to get my life back. My dad eventually agreed to bring my abusive girlfriend up. I cared for her, so I hoped she would get sober, but this was a huge mistake.

For the next eight months, she verbally abused me, degraded, yelled, and hit me. She would only complain, and I mean all the time, so her behavior rubbed off on me until I complained a lot. There was no love from her, so we slept back-to-back almost every day. Honestly, I did not know how to love myself, much less a woman.

This would be the fourth time God would show up. One night I was lying in bed back-to-back with her, and I prayed, "God, please give me a sign that I have not wasted my time and that she cares about me," and before I even said, "Amen," her arm came around my waist. I could not believe this! I was like, "Wow, God, you are good!" This girl did not even have a heart, and here she was holding me. She would call me names that belittled me almost every day because that was her normal. Proverbs 27:15 says, "A quarrelsome wife is as annoying as constant dripping on a rainy day."

When God answered that prayer, it only reassured me what I already knew, and that is how good God is. Seriously, it blew my mind because this woman had not shown me any affection for about three months, besides punching me. That week, for the third time in a week and a half, she came in and jumped on top of me, hitting me. It felt like forty punches in a session here. By the third round of punches, I had a bruise on my arm.

Well, she hit the bruise hard like a man; I flung her off me, and I hit her one time in the eye. It was the first time in thirty-four years I had ever put my hands on a female, and I felt horrible about it. An hour went by, and she started hitting me again. I left this time, and when I got back home; the cops were there; they threw me on the couch and arrested me. I spent thirty days in jail. When I got out, I told my abusive girlfriend she needed to find a way back to Georgia, and I have not seen her since. Thank God!

After I eliminated this toxic person out of my life who was causing me pain, I survived with odd and end construction jobs. It was my last job, and I did not know what I was going to do. I turned to the one that has always been there for me -- God. You will not believe this, but God saved me again when I was two weeks from being homeless.

I had a hard time keeping up with my bills. It was the last day of work on this roof, and I started praying in my head, "God, what do I do? I need a job." Sure enough, that afternoon, Tyson Foods called me, and I had an interview, and for the next four years, I worked at Tyson Foods. I remember thinking this was the second time God gave me a job. I felt so great about my faith that I compared it to a mountain and not the mountain that one looks at as an obstacle, but the kind that is immovable.

I had gotten used to God answering my prayers by now, but I want to say be careful what you pray for. My job was incredibly hard! For a year, I would wake up sore, and I would pray to God, asking Him for all His strength because the job was just physically draining. When my time was up at Tyson, though, I was incredibly grateful. It was a lot of wear and tear on my body. I was also proud of myself for not quitting. I became the best at my job, but I knew it was time to leave there.

After four years, I got fired because I was over my limit of absences, according to the work policy, so I deserved it. Plus, I had an unfiltered mouth and a poor attitude. Tyson was really a huge blessing, not only the physical shape it put me in, but it made my thoughts (that I was ugly) go away. This was one of the greatest gifts God gave me. I had left there unplagued by the thoughts I had since I was thirteen. God removed that powerful lie from my mind, but I still did not know how to communicate with, treat, or trust people. Unfortunately, thirty people got COVID-19 soon after I left the job.

A year earlier, the liberation of communicating these events that had ruined my life, like the sexual abuse, was a huge blessing. We can become so hidden from society because of damaging events in our lives.

I believe God is far better than we deserve, and because He never gives up on us, I love him so much. Earlier in 2019, I went to the store, and a lady was there with her mom and son. They could not afford all the items in their basket, so I purchased the twenty-four pack of water for her because of her two-year-old boy. After I paid for my food, right before I got in my car, she yelled, "Hey, he wants to tell you something." I went over to them, and this two-year-old boy said three words I will never forget: "Love you. Later." I went to my car and cried because I knew he could see my angels.

I am so apologetic to God and everyone else I may have affected by my shameful acts. The tough part was when I decided I would no longer run from my past mistakes. I looked up to heaven and prayed for God's help. Well, again, He came through and answered my prayers.

The power in Jesus' name shows up and shows out when you believe. Matthew 14:36 says, "They begged him to let the sick touch at least the fringe of his robe, and all who touched him were healed." God showed up for me through preachers. These were some of the greatest men and women on the planet, and I am so grateful for God's army of angels that he sent to heal me.

Confusion came over me in the process God took me through. I had never even read a page of the Bible, but I knew it was imperative to keep my faith and trust in Him. God was putting me through the fire only because of my faith in Jesus. Though I had many negative things happen to me, the beauty about Jesus is He kept me unburned only to set me free. Daniel 3:25 says, "Look! Nebuchadnezzar shouted. I see four men, unbound, walking around in the fire unharmed! And the fourth looks like a god!"

CHAPTER 7

A NEW CREATURE IN CHRIST

Social media became a popular way to communicate. I felt insecure because of my negative thoughts about the online world. I heard about many young people committing suicide because of bullying on social media, but again faith will get you through anything.

It is important to be aware of God's presence. There are a couple of things that will go with me to the grave. Those experiences are just for me to keep to myself. There are certain things that other people will not understand because God created the experience just for you. This applies all throughout life. Everyone does not have to know everything about you.

Around June 2020, God said, "Put me in your ears... I love you, son," so I cut off every single person trying to contact me on my phone. No longer did I pay them any attention. I know everything God did for me. He will do the same for you. The transition from rap music to only listening to gospel music, audio bible, and praying all the time was incredible. You can think a prayer, but speaking prayers out loud is more powerful.

God healed my negative thoughts and porn addiction and gave me a smile, which was new. He is still working as I write to you, teaching me to have faith and trust people again. One other fabulous thing God did was to destroy all the reasons I used drugs for twenty-two years. This makes it far easier to say no to drugs. I am going to pass this blessing on to as many people as I can.

Now here I am putting a lifelong list of pain from my head into this testimony. I am using my words to paint you a picture of my journey with God. I pray God uses it to heal people and to give them their smiles back. God wants us smiling again because He loves us that much!

I went on a three-week journey to find some answers, and when I got back home, my roommate had changed all my locks. He became my enemy at that point. The Bible says, "do not do evil for evil," so instead of making him homeless, I signed my apartment over to him after five years of living there. 1 Peter 3:9 says, "Don't repay evil for evil. Don't retaliate with insults when people insult you. Instead, pay them back with a blessing. That is what God has called you to do, and he will grant you his blessing." That is what God has called us to do, and He will grant you blessings. After what God had done for me, I knew I would be okay because God knew what He was doing. That place would have kept me stuck and possibly dead before I knew it. It was time for me to move on.

I had to collect unemployment during this time, but I was grateful for the opportunity to study the Bible, and this is the first time I took the chance to study.

Shortly after giving my place of living up, I stayed with my brother. One day he attacked me, but I had a different reaction this time because I calmly called the police while he was attacking me. I did not yell at him or hit him. I already knew then I had the armor of God, and I did not want to hurt him. Ephesians 6:11 says, "Put on all of God's armor so that you will be able to stand firm against all strategies of the devil." Now, it was time to go, and God led me to Georgia, and I knew why. I had to clean up my past from seven years ago.

I knew I would have to serve some jail time; it was a move that I had to make. I was just waiting to see what would happen next. I spent two months in jail when I got back, and I am currently waiting on the court to keep my past where it belongs… in my past. The devil is still trying to stop me through my family and drugs. I will not let them stop me from writing this and moving forward with whatever it is God has for me. The journey may be a fight, but it is not my fight; it is the Lord's.

Before I end this story of my life, I want to tell you about two events. One of my other aunts had cirrhosis of the liver, and the doctors gave her less than six months to live. She was yellow and could not move off the couch. Through faith and prayer, that was roughly fifteen years ago, and she is still with us today. Thank you so much, God. I wrote this because I know my story can heal others.

A friend of mine named Brandon had done three tours in Iraq. After seven months into our friendship, he told me his story about his military experience. He told me on his third tour, he had to shoot a twelve-year-old boy with a suicide bomb strapped to him. Because he had a nine-year-old at home, it destroyed him mentally and emotionally. I could see this deep pain as he was crying.

When he finished, I thanked him. On my way home, it was this tingle that traveled from my head to my toes. I was thinking, "Is this it, Lord?" It was like the shame, guilt, and depression had lifted off of me. 1 Timothy 4:6 says, "If you explain these things to the brothers and sisters, Timothy, you will be a worthy servant of Christ Jesus, one who is nourished by the message of faith and the good teaching you have followed."

At this point, I knew God had changed my destiny, and it was only the beginning: I want every one of you to know how much I love you all. I pray I make God and all of you proud. You guys mean the world to me.

I pray you will follow these three steps:

1. Pray
2. Audio Bible
3. Gospel music through a set of trusty headphones

People closest to you are the most likely to hurt you, whether they may or may not mean to. I would like to leave you with this blessing from God. I know this because of how He healed me. I want you to remember God is the potter, and we are the clay, so I say one word: #racialequality. If we think it, we will be it.

Today, I am so joyful. I am actually in church sharing and trying to be a light. Who would have thought? Not me! Thank you for reading my story. Psalm 107:2 says, "Has the Lord redeemed you? Then speak out! Tell others he has redeemed you from your enemies."

GIVE ALL GLORY TO GOD!!!

HEALING

Sing, O daughter of Zion;
shout aloud, O Israel!
Be glad and rejoice with all your heart,
O daughter of Jerusalem!

Zephaniah 3:14

For the LORD your God is living among you.
He is a mighty savior.
He will take delight in you with gladness.
With his love, he will calm all your fears.
He will rejoice over you with joyful songs.

Zephaniah 3:17

This is what the LORD says: Be fair-minded and just. Do what is right! Help those who have been robbed; rescue them from their oppressors. Quit your evil deeds! Do not mistreat foreigners, orphans, and widows. Stop murdering the innocent!

Jeremiah 22:3

"For the time is coming,"
says the LORD,
"when I will raise up a righteous descendant
from King David's line.
He will be a King who rules with wisdom.
He will do what is just and right throughout the land.

Jeremiah 23:5

And this will be his name:
The LORD Is Our Righteousness.
In that day Judah will be saved,
and Israel will live in safety.

Jeremiah 23:6

O LORD, if you heal me, I will be truly healed;
if you save me, I will be truly saved.
My praises are for you alone!

Jeremiah 17:14

People scoff at me and say,
"What is this 'message from the LORD' you talk about?
Why don't your predictions come true?"

Jeremiah 17:15

LORD don't terrorize me!
You alone are my hope in the day of disaster.

Jeremiah 17:17

but then that nation renounces its evil ways, I will not destroy it as I had planned.

Jeremiah 18:8

(Quit sinning and doing things that cause us pain.)

O Lord of Heaven's Armies,
you test those who are righteous,
and you examine the deepest thoughts and secrets.
Let me see your vengeance against them,
for I have committed my cause to you.

Jeremiah 20:12

(Your success)

Sing to the Lord!
Praise the Lord!
For though I was poor and needy,
he rescued me from my oppressors.

Jeremiah 20:13

Wise words bring approval,
but fools are destroyed by their own words.

Ecclesiastes 10:12

(Be careful what you say and think about or to yourselves.)

Wise words bring approval,
but fools are destroyed by their own words.

Ecclesiastes 10:13

(What you think about yourself is what you will become.)

But Moses pleaded with the LORD, "O Lord, I'm not very good with words. I never have been, and I'm not now, even though you have spoken to me. I get tongue-tied, and my words get tangled."

Exodus 4:10

Then the LORD asked Moses, "Who makes a person's mouth? Who decides whether people speak or do not speak, hear or do not hear, see or do not see? Is it not I, the LORD?

Exodus 4:11

(It is not just what we say; things we see will also dictate whether we do good or bad)

Now go! I will be with you as you speak, and I will instruct you in what to say."

Exodus 4:12

For the LORD grants wisdom!
From his mouth come knowledge and understanding.

Proverbs 2:6

Wisdom will save you from evil people,
from those whose words are twisted.

Proverbs 2:12

Wisdom will save you from the immoral woman,
from the seductive words of the promiscuous woman.

Proverbs 2:16

(Love can heal or destroy)

But the wicked will be removed from the land,
and the treacherous will be uprooted.

Proverbs 2:22

None of us can hold back our spirit from departing. None of us has the power to prevent the day of our death. There is no escaping that obligation, that dark battle. And in the face of death, wickedness will certainly not rescue the wicked.

Ecclesiastes 8:8

When a crime is not punished quickly, people feel it is safe to do wrong.

Ecclesiastes 8:11

(If you get away with it, you think, I GOT AWAY WITH IT THE FIRST TIME.)

Better to have wisdom than weapons of war,
but one sinner can destroy much that is good.

Ecclesiastes 9:18

Then he said, "You son of the devil, full of every sort of deceit and fraud, and enemy of all that is good! Will you never stop perverting the true ways of the Lord?

Acts 13:10

(Righteousness causes life, and mischief causes death.)

But the apostles stayed there a long time, preaching boldly about the grace of the Lord. And the Lord proved their message was true by giving them power to do miraculous signs and wonders.

Acts 14:3

(Again, our actions must be good deeds.)

Then a mob of Gentiles and Jews, along with their leaders, decided to attack and stone them.

Acts 14:5

And there they preached the Good News.

Acts 14:7

So Paul called to him in a loud voice, "Stand up!" And the man jumped to his feet and started walking.

Acts 14:10

A mob quickly formed against Paul and Silas, and the city officials ordered them stripped and beaten with wooden rods.

Acts 16:22

(Embarrassment will lock you in your mind.)

They were severely beaten, and then they were thrown into prison. The jailer was ordered to make sure they didn't escape.

Acts 16:23

(Putting your hands on someone makes them feel bad, and normally you feel bad. Embarrassment locks you in your mind.)

So, the jailer put them into the inner dungeon and clamped their feet in the stocks.

Acts 16:24

(The mind, your inner prison, can keep you from going out and being all God meant you to be)

Around midnight Paul and Silas were praying and singing hymns to God, and the other prisoners were listening.

Acts 16:25

Suddenly, there was a massive earthquake, and the prison was shaken to its foundations. All the doors immediately flew open, and the chains of every prisoner fell off!

Acts 16:26

(All the negative thoughts changed to positive thoughts.)

But an angel of the Lord came at night, opened the gates of the jail, and brought them out. Then he told them, "Go to the Temple and give the people this message of life!"

Acts 5:19-20

Go to the Temple and give the people this message of life!

Acts 5:20

(The temple is our mind and body, so go inside and think what God thinks about you as well as teach others)

Then someone arrived with startling news: "The men you put in jail are standing in the Temple, teaching the people!"

Acts 5:25

But this is what you must do: Tell the truth to each other. Render verdicts in your courts that are just and that lead to peace.

Zechariah 8:16

Don't scheme against each other. Stop your love of telling lies that you swear are the truth. I hate all these things, says the LORD."

Zechariah 8:17

(Thinking evil will produce evil; thinking good will produce good.)

I will guard my Temple
and protect it from invading armies.
I am watching closely to ensure
that no more foreign oppressors overrun my people's land.

Zechariah 9:8

(When God heals you, be grateful and joyful, and you will never listen to another lie about yourself)

So I concluded there is nothing better than to be happy and enjoy ourselves as long as we can.

Ecclesiastes 3:12
My people are being destroyed
because they don't know me.
Since you priests refuse to know me,
I refuse to recognize you as my priests.
Since you have forgotten the laws of your God,
I will forget to bless your children.

Hosea 4:6

(It is sad to see even the kids in jail.)

You will eat but never have enough.
Your hunger pangs and emptiness will remain.
And though you try to save your money,
it will come to nothing in the end.
You will save a little,
but I will give it to those who conquer you.

Micah 6:14

(Thinking you're better than anyone else)

Therefore, I will wound you!
I will bring you to ruin for all your sins.

Micah 6:13

(Rich people, be careful not to trust in your riches; only trust in God.)

You have planted much but harvest little. You eat but are not satisfied. You drink but are still thirsty. You put on clothes but cannot keep warm. Your wages disappear as though you were putting them in pockets filled with holes!

Haggai 1:6

(Gamblers, drug users, and cheaters are never satisfied.)

But if you stop your sinning and begin to obey the LORD your God, he will change his mind about this disaster that he has announced against you.

Jeremiah 26:13

As for me, I am in your hands - do with me as you think best.

Jeremiah 26:14

But did King Hezekiah and the people kill him for saying this? No, they turned from their sins and worshiped the LORD. They begged him for mercy. Then the LORD changed his mind about the terrible disaster he had pronounced against them. So we are about to do ourselves great harm."

Jeremiah 26:19

While he was speaking, I fainted and lay there with my face to the ground. But Gabriel roused me with a touch and helped me to my feet.

Daniel 8:18

Don't let evil conquer you, but conquer evil by doing good.

Romans 12:21

(This one is difficult, but it is a powerful way to forgive. It can change the other person and keep you from turning evil.)

the creation looks forward to the day when it will join God's children in glorious freedom from death and decay.

Romans 8:21

(God is far better than we can imagine.)

And if the people of Israel turn from their unbelief, they will be grafted in again, for God has the power to graft them back into the tree.

Romans 11:23

(He never gives up on you, this I know!)

But the Lord said, "Go, for Saul is my chosen instrument to take my message to the Gentiles and to kings, as well as to the people of Israel.

Acts 9:15

(We are all chosen by God to be the best we can be)

"'How can you say, "We are wise because we have the word of the LORD," when your teachers have twisted it by writing lies?

Jeremiah 8:8

(Be careful what you read and write, and I will show you why in the next verse)

Esther said, "If it pleases the king, and if I have found favor with him, and if he thinks it is right, and if I am pleasing to him, let there be a decree that reverses the orders of Haman son of Hammedatha the Agagite, who ordered that Jews throughout all the king's provinces should be destroyed.

Esther 8:5

(When we write or read, we need to think, read, and write positive things about ourselves.)

Pray that I will proclaim this message as clearly as I should.

Colossians 4:4

(Invoking that state of mind)

Let the message about Christ, in all its richness, fill your lives. Teach and counsel each other with all the wisdom he gives. Sing psalms and hymns and spiritual songs to God with thankful hearts.

Colossians 3:16

(This is a vital part of the healing process. Remember the words: deep sleep.)

This includes you who were once far away from God. You were his enemies, separated from him by your evil thoughts and actions.

Colossians 1:21

Are any of you suffering hardships? You should pray. Are any of you happy? You should sing praises.

James 5:13

(Extremely vital!)

And a small rudder makes a huge ship turn wherever the pilot chooses to go, even though the winds are strong.

James 3:4

(Notice how a little helm steers the boat.)

In the same way, the tongue is a small thing that makes grand speeches. But a tiny spark can set a great forest on fire.

James 3:5

(Your tongue guides your life and others' lives, so be careful what you say.)

And among all the parts of the body, the tongue is a flame of fire. It is a whole world of wickedness, corrupting your entire body. It can set your whole life on fire, for it is set on fire by hell itself.

James 3:6

(Notice the s on members it is not just our tongue but our actions. The things we hear, see, think, write, and read can also set the course of our lives)

but no one can tame the tongue. It is restless and evil, full of deadly poison.

James 3:8

(We must learn to watch what we say, everyone deserves to smile)

And so blessing and cursing come pouring out of the same mouth. Surely, my brothers and sisters, this is not right!

James 3:10

(If God heals you, blessings will start to come out of your mouth over time)

Does a spring of water bubble out with both fresh water and bitter water?

James 3:11

(This is why some of these preachers should be more careful, and the answer is no)

Words alone will not discipline a servant;
the words may be understood, but they are not heeded.

Proverbs 29:19

(This is why dedication to God is so important.)

A worthy wife is a crown for her husband,
but a disgraceful woman is like cancer in his bones.

Proverbs 12:4

(Love heals or destroys. Nobody wants to go out and have to worry if their better half is cheating on them.)

Stopping her complaints is like trying to stop the wind
or trying to hold something with greased hands.

Proverbs 27:16

(We all know that is impossible.)

When the godly succeed, everyone is glad.
When the wicked take charge, people go into hiding.

Proverbs 28:12

(Come on, world leaders. Get it together!)

But Paul shook off the snake into the fire and was unharmed.

Acts 28:5

(When God heals you, there is nothing that can come near you to destroy you.)

He had the apostle James (John's brother) killed with a sword.

Acts 12:2

(We know the sword is your words.)

When Herod saw how much this pleased the Jewish people, he also arrested Peter. (This took place during the Passover celebration.

Acts 12:3

(When people try to embarrass you in front of a crowd)

The night before Peter was to be placed on trial, he was asleep, fastened with two chains between two soldiers. Others stood guard at the prison gate.

Acts 12:6

(Of course, chains are the things that hinder us and keep us prisoners of our minds)

He motioned for them to quiet down and told them how the Lord had led him out of prison. "Tell James and the other brothers what happened," he said. And then he went to another place.

Acts 12:17

(This is how we know he was killed by words)

As Paul spoke on and on, a young man named Eutychus, sitting on the windowsill, became very drowsy. Finally, he fell sound asleep and dropped three stories to his death below.

Acts 20:9

(God works while you're sleeping.)

Paul went down, bent over him, and took him into his arms. "Don't worry," he said, "he's alive!"

Acts 20:10

(I saw love in this scripture)

Then they all went back upstairs, shared in the Lord's Supper, and ate together. Paul continued talking to them until dawn, and then he left.

Acts 20:11

(God works while you are sleeping and awake. Jesus is the bread.)

Meanwhile, the young man was taken home alive and well, and everyone was greatly relieved.

Acts 20:12

It's better to live alone in the corner of an attic
than with a quarrelsome wife in a lovely home.

Proverbs 21:9

(Fighting and love will destroy as well.)

A quarrelsome wife is as annoying
as constant dripping on a rainy day.

Proverbs 27:15

(Cheating equals a broken heart like a leaky roof destroys a home.)

Commit yourself to instruction;
listen carefully to words of knowledge.

Proverbs 23:12

(God is the potter, and we are the clay)

Direct your children onto the right path,
and when they are older, they will not leave it.

Proverbs 22:6

(Plant the seed early because kids' brains are sponges. We know that.)

for I am giving you good guidance.
Don't turn away from my instructions.

Proverbs 4:2

(Please know and understand God loves us all.)

My father taught me,
"Take my words to heart.
Follow my commands, and you will live.

Proverbs 4:4

My child, pay attention to what I say.
Listen carefully to my words.

Proverbs 4:20

Avoid all perverse talk;
stay away from corrupt speech.

Proverbs 4:24

Wisdom will multiply your days
and add years to your life.

Proverbs 9:11

The fears of the wicked will be fulfilled;
the hopes of the godly will be granted.

Proverbs 10:24

(Thinking positive, not worrying)

The mouth of the godly person gives wise advice,
but the tongue that deceives will be cut off.

Proverbs 10:31

(You can actually lock your own self up by your words and thoughts.)

The LORD detests evil plans,
but he delights in pure words.

Proverbs 15:26

If you repay good with evil,
evil will never leave your house.

Proverbs 17:13

(Use God's love; it is the only way.)

If you repay good with evil,
evil will never leave your house.

Proverbs 17:27

The mouths of fools are their ruin;
they trap themselves with their lips.

Proverbs 18:7

The tongue can bring death or life;
those who love to talk will reap the consequences.

Proverbs 18:21

Does not my word burn like fire?"
says the LORD.
"Is it not like a mighty hammer
that smashes a rock to pieces?

Jeremiah 23:29

That is why I tell you not to worry about everyday life - whether you have enough food and drink, or enough clothes to wear. Isn't life more than food, and your body more than clothing?

Matthew 6:25

(Worrying keeps us trapped.)

Can all your worries add a single moment to your life?

Matthew 6:27

And why worry about your clothing? Look at the lilies of the field and how they grow. They don't work or make their clothing,

Matthew 6:28

So don't worry about these things, saying, 'What will we eat? What will we drink? What will we wear?'

Matthew 6:31

So don't worry about tomorrow, for tomorrow will bring its own worries. Today's trouble is enough for today.

Matthew 6:34

(That is six times in nine scriptures the word worry is used. We stay stuck if we worry.)

Yes, I will certainly keep you safe from these wicked men. I will rescue you from their cruel hands."

Jeremiah 15:21

(You have to believe that is that.)

Do not get married or have children in this place.

Jeremiah 16:2

(Unhappy marriages destroy the relationship and the kids.)

For this is what the LORD says about the children born here in this city and about their mothers and fathers:

Jeremiah 16:3

They will die from terrible diseases. No one will mourn for them or bury them, and they will lie scattered on the ground like manure. They will die from war and famine, and their bodies will be food for the vultures and wild animals."

Jeremiah 16:4

(Bad relationships trap kids from being all they are supposed to be.)

With their words, the godless destroy their friends,
but knowledge will rescue the righteous.

Proverbs 11:9

Upright citizens are good for a city and make it prosper,
but the talk of the wicked tears it apart.

Proverbs 11:11

It is foolish to belittle one's neighbor;
a sensible person keeps quiet.

Proverbs 11:12

Evil people will surely be punished,
but the children of the godly will go free.

Proverbs 11:21

The wicked are trapped by their own words,
but the godly escape such trouble.

Proverbs 12:13

Some people make cutting remarks,
but the words of the wise bring healing.

Proverbs 12:18

Those who control their tongue will have a long life;
opening your mouth can ruin everything.

Proverbs 13:3

Do what is good and run from evil
so that you may live!
Then the LORD God of Heaven's Armies will be your helper,
just as you have claimed.

Amos 5:14

(Do good. Speak righteously.)

You make vows and break them;
you kill and steal and commit adultery.
There is violence everywhere -
one murder after another.

Hosea 4:2

(These things are breaking someone's heart, hurting them and you.)

Do not let any part of your body become an instrument of evil to serve sin. Instead, give yourselves completely to God, for you were dead, but now you have new life. So use your whole body as an instrument to do what is right for the glory of God.

Romans 6:13

(The tongue is referred to as a member but notice the s. It is not just what you speak; it is what you hear, think, see, etc. The pathway to heaven is narrow.)

They know the truth about God because he has made it obvious to them.

Romans 1:19

(If you think about it and put it into action, you will accomplish it. Believe you can do all things through Jesus.)

Dear brothers and sisters, when troubles of any kind come your way, consider it an opportunity for great joy.

James 1:2

(There is always a lesson learned you can pass on to the younger generations.)

For the word of God is alive and active. Sharper than any double-edged sword, it penetrates even to dividing soul and spirit, joints, and marrow; it judges the thoughts and attitudes of the heart.

Hebrews 4:12

(Now we know words do hurt.)

I have not run away from being your shepherd;
you know I have not desired the day of despair.
What passes my lips is open before you.

Jeremiah 17:16

The LORD is good,
a refuge in times of trouble.
He cares for those who trust in him,

Nahum 1:7

If you want to smile when God heals you, there is no going back. You, too, will be joyful! God will take every reason in your mind away that causes you to get high or be unhappy!

Time for action: This will be different for everyone, but I did this for five months, twenty-four hours a day. It will not take you long to remember you are worth it. Remember, deep sleep. I love you more than life itself. Please smile again; God loves you so much!

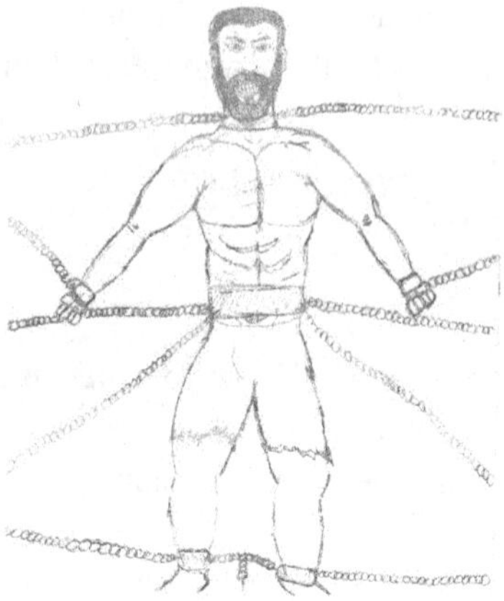

"If your spirit is low, no matter what you have in life, you will be sad, but if your spirit is high no matter where you are at in life, you will be happy!"

- NATHAN DYER

"If you remember what God has done for you, it is easy to forget what has been done to you!"

- NATHAN DYER

CPSIA information can be obtained
at www.ICGtesting.com
Printed in the USA
LVHW012232180521
687790LV00014B/1374

9 780578 908427